Words on love, loss, and longing

Dark Little Corners

DARK LITTLE CORNERS

Poems and Proses

SHUBHAM SINGHANIA

Sometimes even all the lights out there couldn't

extinguish the darkness inside you

Author's Note

When I started writing, only a few people knew that I wrote. My words were not particularly happy or inspiring, but more about sadness, silences, and negative thoughts. A few years back, I was going through my darkest times in life, and writing helped make life easier. So, I created an Instagram page under the username *@poorbrokenguy (pbg)* and shared my thoughts. It was easier to be vulnerable and sad while remaining anonymous.

I felt ashamed whenever someone used to say my username loud. Over time, I accepted the name and learned to embrace the vulnerability that comes with it and with my writings.

It took me a long time to accept that these words were worthy of being published in a book. As I write this, I still struggle with them, but I am getting there, slowly and steadily. I understand that life is a big painting filled with all kinds of emotions, and this book looks into the messy, sloppy, dark colours that often stay hidden in the corners and make the painting more alive.

I hope that as you navigate through these colours through the words in this book, they bring you comfort and a hope that there is light at the end of tunnel, no matter how intense the void, numbness and choke may be.

Shubham (- pbg)
Bangalore, 3rd May 2024

PART I

void

the state of being without you

"Hi, how are you? Do ..

Well, I already have tears in my eyes. My lips are unconsciously stretching to fake a smile, the only thing I have learned in the past few months without you. They are dry and burnt, so it won't taste like it did before.

Yes, I was going to ask, how are you doing? I mean, do you miss me? Even just a bit?

I know you do. But I do more. See, I won. I always told you I loved you more. The trophy I won, though, is hidden. No one can see it. Not even me, sometimes. In those moments, I avoid everything and everyone.

I live alone with my cell phone, and my nights are full of darkness and silence. The tears have dried up. I rarely sleep, and my skin is peeling off. The memories are just a matter of old times now.

I have also accepted that you are gone, and I don't have you in my destiny. What I failed to realise all this time is that the life I am living is my trophy. I have won it for loving you more than anything. All I ever wanted was to see you smile forever.

The thing is that
I am still waiting at the station,
and you have boarded the train.

The more I seek relief,
the harder it punches me in the face.
It makes me realize
how fragile I am without you.

Often, I wonder..
whether the lines on my palm,
meeting and then parting ways,
depict us?

I will bury my pain so deep in my heart
that no one will be able to see it
in my eyes anymore.

The void in my life
due to your absence is painful.
It suffocates me
without any rope around my neck,
even when I breathe.

Your skin is the closest
I have been to God.

Nothing has changed since you were gone.

I have the same job to do, the usual place for my coffee, and the same old friends to talk to. It's just that life wasn't hard when you were close to my skin.

But now, it hurts deep inside to live the same old life with bruises on my heart, all alone, without you by my side.

Half-detached soul

She accepted me with my heart, no matter how childish it was. She never judged me by my actions or appearance. She loved my weak heart. I always knew that we didn't have much time together, so we stopped thinking about future. I left everything in my life just to be with her. We made countless memories in whatever time we had. We wandered through cities all day and partied until midnight. We travelled together, spending our days on beaches and nights in each other's arms. There was not a single day when she didn't confess how much she loved me. I always thought that I would be fine. But during all this, I never realised that these memories would be the only thing that would haunt me. I made her my love, my parents, healer, counsellor, soulmate, God, and my entire universe. I never realized when I lost my own shadow to her. My day started with her thoughts and I fell asleep in her arms, dreaming about her. When I walked, I always saw my hand holding hers. When I ate, my plate was always prepared to serve her. When confused, my mind sought her for suggestions. When I slept, my head always had her shoulder to lean on. I don't know when my soul merged into hers and became one. But now, after losing her, I feel nothing. My heart is lost somewhere in the dark. My mind follows the rules laid down by the people around me. My eyes keep playing flashes of our memories in the back, with a silent fake smile hiding in the loud scream inside me. And my body is just carrying my bleeding soul, detached from her.

The question is not
how far you will go for your love,
but rather
how much pain
you can bear for her happiness.

More stories will be written. Some will be repeated, and some will be erased. As weeks will become months and months into years, every story we wrote together will become old.

The words once written will fade away.

There will be new memories and a new story to write on the same old paper. Yet no matter how beautiful your story may be, the ink traces of my love will always stand beside you, in disguise, smiling and content in your happiness.

I don't want to forget you ever. Because even now the feeling of loving you is far more soothing than the pain of losing you.

Together we could have a wonderful life giggling and having each other in our hardest time.

But even without you, it's not that bad.

It is just that I will always miss you beside me and my eyes will be the first one to speak about it.

I never craved for sex as much as I yearned for physical intimacy between us.

Holding your hand, gently grazing your skin with my fingertips, stroking your hair, cuddling in the dark, your cheek pressed softly against my chest, and then a kiss on your forehead before we fall asleep.

Love is always about more of these things, isn't it?

This love has blossomed on drugs. It is deep-rooted in my nerves. I have seen nothing but your love at the end of this world. It is heaven and it is hell for me.

A single day spent with you has always felt like a month, and during our time together, we lived a whole lifetime. We have walked down the aisle and even survived the fire beneath our feet, holding each other's hand.

Now tell me, after all of this, how will I be able to survive alone without you?

Is there any thread left between us
that I can tie off
to get you back?

Withdrawal

You are still not getting it. I still have not accepted that I have to live this life without you. There is still a hope in my heart, but in reality, you are long gone.

That you are tied to someone else for life.

And when I realise this, I feel a stillness in my heart as if it has stopped beating.

"Please, I don't want to lose her," my heart whispers.

I cannot bear this loneliness. I want to survive it, but it is eating me from inside. I am losing it. I am scared. And there is no one to save me. I need you. Desperately.

This pain is getting unbearable from a few days. I can see you and him moving forward, and I am still standing here where you left me. I am scared and tired of life in your absence.

I wonder what my reason for the pain is and why God did this to me. If you were to go, why did he bring us together and show us the path to each other's hearts?

I cannot live without you. I am doing everything I should to move on, but my heart only thinks about you. I feel disconnected from my heart when I am not with you. It's like I am not breathing at all. My body feels like a dead person, and my heart cries out for your love.

I am trying my best. But if someday this pain takes over me and I die out here alone without you, please don't hesitate to come close to me.

My body would still be craving for your hug and my lips waiting for your kiss to set my soul free.

Someday this pain will also end, though with me.

Soul's Remorse 23

Again their souls
have to wait
for another life to be together
because they chose wrong body to dwell upon.

When I folded my hands to pray,
I asked for nothing else but you.
I only wished to spend this life with you,
your hand holding mine,
and your head resting on my shoulder.

I did everything in my capacity to have you close in my arms. I sacrificed everything dear to me. And here I stand once again, right in front of you, calling for you to hold my hand. I am ready to fight anyone who tries to tear us apart. I will make everything right. I will not let the smile fade away from your pretty face. Forever. I promise.

But despite all this, God chose him over me for you. Why would he do something like this to me? I am not that bad!

I am sorry for whatever I have done. Please stop this pain.

I guess,
God never had
his share of heartbreak.
Otherwise,
he would not have
created a heart for us.

The best thing about being broken
is that now I can endure any amount of pain.

The creator of this universe
took my universe away from me.
And so, I will defy him
and everything he has touched.

He is a fucker and no longer exists to me.
I will not look at his face.
He has seen my love and devotion;
now he will see my hate.
It doesn't matter whether it affects him or not.

He wanted a game,
so I challenge him:
Let's see how much pain
you can give me now.

This surely looks like God's hell to me. I feel this unbearable pain in my heart every time I breathe. Deep inside, my soul is shouting in a closed, dark room with the pain of losing you to someone else. It shamelessly begs in my dreams to return what has been taken away from it.

Some fates are just nothing,

but amongst the ill-conceived creations of God.

In the search of love,
I have lost my way.

Distances Between Us

You are not as close to him
as you were to me.

And I am closer to you
than he is to you.

And you are less closer to me
than you have ever been.

I wish we could all go back to where we were

I don't fear him kissing you on your lips. I don't mind you making out with him.

It's not that I don't feel anything; I do.

But knowing you are okay, and I am yours forever is more important to me. The only thing I am scared of is your feelings—that they will change, that you will start loving him more than me. I cannot lose that.

You will not miss me
when you tie your life with him,
but you will remember me
when he makes love to you.

My lips,
my hands,
how I caressed your body,
the feeling that I loved you,
and of my lips pressed against yours—
you will miss every bit of it.

Maybe they are right — that there must be something better for me than you. But they don't understand that this heart only seeks you. There is no replacement, no matter how much better it may be. I don't want anything good without you by my side. But there is no amount of pain I can tolerate or tears I can shed that can bring you back.

Another night without you

Do you know how scratching the wound feels like?

It makes me realise how incomplete I am without you and how badly I miss you. When your hand touched mine, my bruised heart ached with relief. I wanted to be loved once again. I wished all the days I spent without you to be a bad dream. The rage inside me was no more there, and your kiss brought me back to life.

But when you are really gone, all I feel is more vulnerable, broken, and how much poor I am to afford you.

I am not afraid of moving on. I am not afraid of going out and being around people to live a good life. However, what I am truly afraid of is more love and pain that might come with it.

If there is love, there will be pain, and my heart knows that I cannot tolerate more of it. I have reached my peak point, and even a small trigger could burst me out. All the screams I have locked away in the cage would break free, and there would be no more "me" living out here.

Either I will die or there will be a psychopath bathing in the blood of people who hurt me in the past. So, instead of stitching my wounds, I prefer to keep them fresh and open, so that my body and soul continue to ache for you, and I can keep my screams locked away in the cage forever.

Imperfections

I love you, not because you are a perfect person, but because of who you truly are—the person you hide from everyone else. The one I find more beautiful than anything. The one I would choose again and again over anything else. The silly things you do, your anger issues, your insecurities—what you call flaws, I see as perfectly normal. I see them as being the real 'you'. Those are the things that make you unique; that make you 'mine'.

I don't want you to be like others, trying to fit in someone's else shoes. And I am not being too humble or compromising, because I am not perfect either.

My soul felt fulfilled when I saw your smile for the first time. The times when you are not yourself, I love to hold you and make you believe in *'us'*. These are the bonds I have made with your unique self, the parts you call your imperfections. For me, those are the beautiful, pesky bits of you that make me fall in love with you even more. I don't want to lose a single one of them. I want to embrace them as I hold you during cold nights, resting in my arms, close to my heart.

Your imperfections make me fall in love with you even more.

Your smile is so contagious.

I saw it once,

and it made me return back to normal in a snap.

You know why I smoke cigarettes.
Because sometimes it feels good
to burn all the memories
popping in the head
and suffocating me
every time I breathe.

Whenever I try to step outside from the cage of your love,
your voices echo in my head
forcing me to crawl back to my prison again.

I whispered to the stars
to whisper
to you
about the whispers
of my heart.

Every morning when the ocean wakes up, he searches for her footprints on his shore.

Did she visit him while he was asleep? Even if she did, his fate won't let him know of her presence.

Dark Little Corners

I crave for your arms every single night, to hold you close to me. I seek the comfort that used to soothe me to sleep.

When I crawl into bed, I find myself utterly lonely and miserable. My skin urges for your touch and my eyes search for your presence. Before I used to tuck a pillow around my arms and hug it tightly, with my blanket rolled up to feel you, but as days pass, my heart is rejecting this deception too.

Now, the only thing left for me is to keep staring at the ceiling in the pitch-black darkness of my room, until my heavy and tired eyes catch a glimmer of light through the window, finally guiding me to the path of peace.

I experience heaven
in your smile;
it is the only thing
that liberates me
from myself.

But ever since you are gone,
I am again caged by my own thoughts.

My wings are clipped,
and the wounds all over my body
are now patiently waiting
for my embrace of death.

Souvenirs

45

I love you in bits and pieces,
carving shadows of them
one-by-one, on my heart

And like souvenirs: I cherish them.

I adore each one of them differently,
so that if one day my heart decided to
un-love any one of them,
I will still have a million others to love.

a million years to un-love

If I leave you,
won't I be leaving a part of myself too?
Just like you left a part of yourself with me
when you said goodbye, that I embrace every night.

Dear..

I wish I could relive all the moments we shared, from our first date to the final goodbye. I want to hold the time and scroll backward to the start of everything. I want to hold your hand again, and walk along the long, pretty beach in the evening, and kiss you passionately under dark moon nights.

I wish you would get sick again, just so I could take care of you all night and take a worrisome nap by your bed. I want to take morning showers with you and receive the first stamp of your lipstick before heading out. The times when I slept away from your arms, I wish I could return to the middle of the night and hug you tight. I want to confess, over and over, how much I love you, and it is only you who makes me smile and happy. I am also sorry for the times I was mean, disrespectful and difficult to handle.

And I also want to say that I need you. I need you to turn around from whatever path you have walked to and hug me like we used to and keep me there because I can't find solace elsewhere than your arms.

The Last Picture

They loved taking pictures of their reflections in the mirror because they, mostly he, wanted to keep those pictures as memories on his phone. He knew that a picture of both of them together would never make it to any bedroom wall; neither his, nor hers, and certainly not theirs. Each time they bid goodbye, before checking out from the hotel room, he used to call her in front of a mirror and pull her close to his arms to take a picture of the moment. That was his way to save her permanently in his life—atleast in the little life he had left.

The first time when he clicked a picture; it was more awkward than he thought. She was not comfortable being close to him, permanently, in a picture. Like all new couples, they also had their boundaries regarding how much they were opening up to each other. His boundary was a few inches less than hers. But like her, he was also not sure if she was the one with whom he wanted to share his vulnerable side.

Over time, however, he realised what others meant by the word "magic of love". It smashed the thick walls they created around themselves and each second they spent with one another was one step closer towards the core of their hearts. Just a few weeks ago, they barely knew each other, but now, they weren't even two different individuals at all.

From his diary, six weeks after their first date:

I think love is like a key maker of anyone's home. If given to one person, it can unlock that person's home. Once the key has been handed over to you, you are allowed to go inside and touch and play with every small or large, open or hidden thing in the house. Also, you always have a choice to stay or leave the home. However, if you choose to leave then the only way to do it is to shatter every piece you had touched or played into unrecognisable pieces. In case you decide to stay, you eventually get comfortable, as if the home that belonged to someone else is now owned by you.

The day they took their last picture was the day he saw her for the last time. She effortlessly swayed to his arms, kissed his cheek, and buried her head in his shoulder. Unlike the first few pictures, he didn't have to pull her. However, those days something additional accompanied her hug. *Tears.* They had become an unavoidable part of their life. Both of their homes were on the verge of collapse. The only thing left by them was to set their foot outside of each other's wrecked homes. He tried to record and capture all such beautiful moments in pictures assuming them to be the last one.

Two years after that day, he found one such picture among the things he hid in a memory box. Looking at it, he realised that the things the pictures fail to capture often become the best memories. Like the huge smoke of sadness covered in both of their eyes. They both were smiling, they had to. It was their last mirror picture. However, despite their efforts to hide everything behind their smiles, there was a visible contradiction between their eyes and smiles and body posture.

He never thought that he could ever feel a pinch of sadness while holding her close, but he doesn't remember exactly when his happiest feeling changed to the saddest one. It didn't land on his heart out of nowhere. The change was progressive. The first time he felt that was when they both gave up on each other. As days passed, the feeling multi-folded. He never fully understood the torment of it until the day he was left all alone, away from the comfort of her arms. The sadness, the collapse of his home and the loneliness after leaving hers, all were clearly visible in his eyes in that last picture. He didn't cry with her that day. He was lost somewhere but awake to her tears and the promises they made for loving each other for forever.

After their last picture, she left, but the smoke of that sadness of her returning all the gifts she admired, the waving of her hands before she vanished in the crowd, and the loneliness inside—they never departed from his eyes.

PART II

numb

the state of not feeling anything

It's all good here,
Don't go anywhere.
    I don't want you to go.

Don't look away,
We will reach there, slow
Don't leave me here, alone,
I can't breathe anymore.
    I'm lost somewhere.

You broke every inch of this heart,
shattered me in pieces,
left them to haunt me all these years.
    And yet

The pieces want you bad,
I need you like a mad.
    Don't forget me.

I will love you more.
Don't go far,
I am coming slow.
Wait,
like I waited for you,
    all my life.

I am lost in you,
drowning myself,
little by little
in the moments
where you belong only to me.

My words scream your name
and hug you close,
yet cannot find the essence of you.

Intentions

If you wanted,
I would have left everything
to be with you.

But the truth is that
you never wanted
to be with me.

Time has passed for you and I both.
I have spent it
remembering you
and you have spent it
forgetting me.

I wonder:
if the time laughs at me, or
feels pity for me.

Cracks Within

It's almost midnight,
and I wish
I don't lose the hope of you coming back.
But you told me to let go
and I wish you didn't mean that.

Everything will be alright:
I wish I could tell you that.
But you told me to notice what I am missing
and I wish you didn't mean that.

I thought we had all the love
to go through all highs and lows.
I wish it was enough.
I wish I was enough for you.

You are my friend,
you are my love,
soul-by-soul
my only place of home;

In the dark days,
you are my partner
and a fiend in the wild nights;

What else you can be;
a broken piece of my heart,
    or a beautiful dream
never meant to complete.

A home I built

All the pretty lights in my home
are just broken glasses on the floor.
I pulled out one stuck in my heart,
and in the agony,
I fled my home.

While I was searching for new ones:
someone moved in and took over my home,
fixed the lights,
and sang her favourite songs,
told gentle words,
and loved her even more.

My heart was lit up with fire,
smoked up till the end,
and then thrown and crushed
like a burnt-cigarette-bud.

Photograph

In flesh you are there,
in the open space of that terrace,
the camera captured you holding his hand
swinging slowly,
staring in his eyes with a soft smile,
looking forward to a beautiful family
and a loving partner.

But I don't know why
my eyes can't recognise the person in the picture.
    This smile: It's fake.

You don't smile like this,
or probably I have never made you happy enough
for a smile beautiful like this.

And one day I will also get tired
of everything I do for you.
I'd question myself
the hours I have spent;
Were they worth it?

And one day I will also forget
how your kiss felt on my lips
and how your love touched my heart

And one day I will also stop waiting for you,
and sleep in peace on my bed,
putting the memory box in the hidden cupboard

And one day I will remember you
after a dozen of drinks in a bar,
going through the old pictures,
and realizing how happy you are in your recent ones.

Caged Bird

In the world of lovers,
I am the lost one watching you from afar,
wrapped in a bedsheet.

You rolled out of bed,
your hair tousled and lipstick messed up.
He again invaded my *home* last night
and you kissed him with passion.
Night after night,
I watched love blossoming between the sheets,
and over time,
the silence of your heart
turning into soft moans,
and with them,
I heard my heart cracking an inch more.

Now in the fading memories,
you don't see me anymore.
And yet I reached out to hold you,
but your arms—they were tightly knit
in a new forever with him.
All these months, I waited on the sidelines silently,
hoping one day you would utter my name.

Even your hug now seems like a long-distant past,
and inside my heart,
your love feels herself like a-caged-bird.

So for the last time,
I breathed in your scent as deeply as I could.
I feed your love,
trinkets of my broken heart
and in the evening
I will collect my baggage from your place.

But before saying you a final goodbye
I write this note,
believing that it will remind you of me,
and you will hide it
in a corner of your home
which I can still call
mine,
    mine, and
        only mine.

Red Towel 65

Nothing so far has given me the solace that I am looking in your absence—neither those countless burning cigarettes that I inhaled to burn myself, nor the cloth around my neck sucking the life out of me.

When I gaze at the stars
in the night,
I wonder
if the stars look at me,
and beg me to stop
the silent screams deafening their ears.

i wonder if they can hear me.

Searching for cut marks on my skin
to prove my love,
but couldn't find any;
when looked in the mirror,
saw myself standing in a pool of blood,
and my blood-soaked heart
ripped out of my chest
lying as a souvenir
to entertain the crowd in a grand circus.

These sober eyes drowning in the lake of sorrow;
as the day passes they keep sinking down,
one inch at a time
in the hope that
someday it will hit the bottom
and then
the water won't be suffocating,
the numbness won't hurt the way it does,
and someday it will feel the peace again.

I do not dream when I sleep.
I keep switching
between
what I had
and what I lost

you are past and present

You either
bury your love in peace,
or love long enough
to see yourself
becoming helpless in love.

"I have been cast out from her heart,
*   and now I have nowhere else to go."*

There was a time when it was so easy to express my feelings, but the words now seem pointless because they failed to do what they were meant for; to bring you back. I don't see you, either in my dreams or when I am awake. The only thing I have is your absence, which I feel almost all of the time. I can't sit silently listening to soothing songs; they make me helpless, and without any hesitation, my heart cries out loud, sobbing in my room.

Previously, I used to soothe him with thoughts that everything would be fine, and I can stay without you:

"It's not love and just fling."

But now, he knows that I was lying, and you are not here. There is so much pain of losing someone so close. I find my crying heart asking you, "Why did you give me so much pain?"

I find myself literally begging in front of you to take this pain away with you as well.

I still cling to the hope that before I let you go, you would come back someday and tell me how badly you missed me, just like I did.

"Like dark night sky waiting for moon."

You would confess that you are not ready to forget me and move on. You would not stop telling me about how you spent the entire night staring at our pictures together and reliving all the memories. You would confess that every night you went to bed without me, my thoughts never skipped your mind. You would hug me tight as if you also had craved for it during all these months. You would promise me that you wanted to stay this time, no matter what, and it would be "us" again.

I think I will never forget you. But I am trying to forget how happy I used to be with you. Because the feeling of the lost happiness takes me back to the first place we met in a hope to live our love story again.

And every time I reached there, I found withered memories fading before my eyes, and the story I lived again wasn't the one where you were waiting impatiently for me in a small café. Rather, it always was me sitting in a corner of my room, hugging my knees, and lost indefinitely in a deep black pit of sadness.

The needles at your house were sharp enough.
I almost started feeling things.

numb

If he goes

She holds his heart in her soft palm
and let its sharp edges make cuts;
    small ones that go unnoticed

Except whenever he comes close,
his touch caresses her bare skin
and a sharp pain trickles down
from the corner of her eyes,
running through her cheeks
to the shivering corners of her lips.

It's been weeks
since her heart has been paralysed
from wrenching coldness
of her unloved bones
that's why her hand desperately pulls him close;
    uncountable cuts across her body
bleed red on his white linen shirt.

"A colour of love, pain and sacrifice," she said.
"Also the unwashable stains", he replied
after a warm embrace.

I inhale the insanity inside her
to keep my sanity intact
till her arms have engulfed mine

And she keeps licking
the wound bites on my skin,
while inflicting some more elsewhere
for her next visit.

On my way back

I opened my closet of memories and took out a multi-dose vial and carefully broke the seal. From the pile of dust, I searched for a syringe, inserted the needle into the rubber tap of the vial, and kept drawing the love poison until the syringe was overloaded. I tied a rubber band on my hand and waited for my blood to fil in the veins. Then I inserted the needle into my vein and injected every drop of your love into my body at once.

Blood was dripping, but who cares, I can see you holding my hand again. I can see us together again forever loving each other.

She visited last night, it seems, when I was asleep. The footprints have been erased, but I can feel her smell inside my blanket, in my arms, and on my lips. She probably came to kiss me goodbye. But I don't want to say goodbye, not yet.

Her traces are fading away with the fresh morning air around me in the sunlight. And I can't stop it. If someone can, please do it now. She is going away. I don't want to lose her… again.

Dry Leaves

I had a desire to
travel across the ocean,
explore the deserts.
But how long
I will scrape your memories
to fly with my severed wings.

Will you help me in getting
the ashes of this body —
    so that when the storm comes,
I can whisper my last words
and travel far away,
drifting for eternity around the globe.

Every morning when I get up,
I try to recollect
the memories of last night,
and recall
how breathless I was without you.

I still can't feel my heart.
But I try to keep moving forward
with the hope
of having
everything right in the future,
only to fail miserably
by the end of the day.

I am like the Autumn's dry leaves:
faded, yet strong,
falling to the call of wind
for the search of spark
to burn and crackle loud
in the agony of separation.

Being the Light

I had dreamed of a life where we are together in each other's arms, roaming cities, having private candlelight dinners, and showing you my love. But all of them have vanished. A part of it is still there somewhere deep inside, but the suffocation that comes with imagining you fulfilling all the dreams with someone else has mostly taken over.

Though whenever I see a happy couple enjoying without worrying about tomorrow, I see you in them living those moments. It reminds me of the loneliness in my life and how miserable it is without you. I imagine how complete it would be if I'd be in his place. All the flashes of the time I spent with you, which I have turned off for good, come back as if they have never left. They remind me how happy and complete we were together and the fact that I won't be able to come that close to you again in my life. It forces my tears to burst open from its shell and puts me again in a position where I curse my existence in this world.

My life revolved around you and ever since you have been taken away from me, I have nowhere to go and nobody to tend to who can understand me. I often question the creator that how he can be so deaf that he didn't listen to any of our prayers. Every time I bowed my head, I had only wished to have a life with you. Only one wish that also remained unfulfilled.

I know many people lose their love, and time heals them. But mine was different. Everyone knows that. We both loved each other from the deepest core of our heart. We both found a common thread that bound us as if we were two parts of one single soul that were separated in previous lives. And these are not clichés. We were never destined to meet but fate brought us together, and it was that who deliberately positioned the magnet between us so that we keep getting back to each other.

That magnet is still there, and I am scared that someday this obsession of your presence in my life will consume me. The pain of losing you has taken away everything from me. My face has lost its smile, my eyes have lost its glow, and my skin has lost its moisture. I am a dead man with regular heartbeats. No medical machine can measure the pain I am enduring. Instead of this, it is much better to just lie breathless on the floor with this half-detached soul. The only thing left with me is this bleeding heart with chronic wounds and some old dry scars. Can you please pray to your dear God to take away this too? Because this pain consumes me in the same way darkness consumes light every day without fail, and I don't want to be the light to bear this suffering everyday till eternity.

It is said that light drives out darkness. But is it easy to be the light? To be defeated by the darkness all the time again and again. To be at his mercy and wait for it to play with yourself brutally till it is done with you and leave you feeling scared, ashamed, and alone, plagued by flashbacks of last night's onslaught, but still keep shining for others.

PART III

choke

the state of being suffocated

Those were the exact words she used when I wrote her my first letter. After that, I only shared them with a limited set of eyes. A week earlier, she was back in town, and was here again, after four years, eight months and nineteen days. The table we used to eat our takeout was thrown away in a corner of my room.

"Our table is broken," she said.

We bought it from a nearby supermarket during the Christmas sale. The shelf was dusting with the stack of old notebooks.

"Those letters. Where are they?"

And it has been a while since I felt a crack in my rib, as if it had been busted from within. Even breathing seemed to hurt. I tried to contain it, but it was as if a tsunami had hit me, and I was airborne; my eyes were closed, and at supersonic speed, I was being pulled towards her arms.

"Everywhere, they are everywhere," I replied, my throat choking, my hands shaking.

"Like ghosts – haunting me, Like yearnings – nourishing me. Like fire – consuming me, Like my bones – supporting me..

Like you – pulling me."

I want to dig a hole in my head and pull your memories out of it. Like a bug, these memories are ruining everything my mind is trying to process. I can't write, I can't love anyone, I can't feel for you anymore. It seems like I am also forgetting your face, and I can't stop that either.

There are moments when I want to open the window of my room and fly high into the sky. But even after seeing the lush green beauty outside and feeling the soft light on my soul, I can't embrace the life outside of this red-stained castle of mine.

Sometimes I feel a gaping hole inside me, filled with things I want to say to you. I have tried to talk about them, but they usually come out as long pauses, or a smile of acceptance, or wide-open eyes of silence. I had even thought of writing about them, but I am not sure how to write about something that I have no words to explain. I even doubt whether they exist for real, or if they are just an illusion created by the loneliness surrounding me.

Sometimes more than anything,
I miss my own presence around me.

Where did all the butterflies and bugs go?

He never liked the fading of leaves and withering of flowers in his garden. To prevent that, he watered his plants on a daily basis and exposed them to proper sunlight as per their requirements. He took care of them in the best possible manner—yet every morning when he woke up, he found green leaves turning yellow and colourful flowers becoming pale. He never quite understood how, but he felt the pain of those leaves and flowers in his heart.

One day, the pain became uncontrollable, and he had to go and get his garden cleaned and cement the floor so that no flower could come to life again. Now, he comfortably sits in a chair on the cemented floor and tries to smile while staring at the sunlight.

I have made peace with pieces of mine
that are slowly dying without you.
Though some of them still complain
but they don't get it;
It's better for them to die
so that no one can hurt them anymore.

Moon
Sky
Water
Sand
You
Me
And the night
A beautiful night

(repeats in my head)

That's it, I don't remember more.

What did we do?
How long did we kiss?
What did we talk about?
    Nothing comes to my mind
As if it was a dream
in which I only remember about things around me

The answer to "who were we" is like:
    Erased.

Broken boat
in a barren lake
search miles
for its parts
and a stream of water
from where it can float back to the river.

In your absence

My words may sound hateful, but they still belong to you, just as I belong to you. At 1 AM, as I stare at the stars and close my eyes, I can still picture us: sitting together, sipping tea in the evening at our usual stall, with you gently pulling the cigarette from my fingers. "I miss that," he, *my heart*, whispers.

Previously, he would shout with anger or go into yet another episode of depression, but now, he is calm. He keeps his sorrows to himself, and the eyes and the heart, they rarely talk. But I know this: on a weekend when there is nothing to keep his thoughts at bay, he hopes to see you. He doesn't dream about impossible, but only small things, like exchanging a few words, or reminding the eyes of your smile.

I have tried everything to convince him; wrote hateful poems, ignored you multiple times even when he specifically warned me that if did that, he will stop talking to me—and he did.

Sometimes I wish that if you could personally convince him. That you are not "his" anymore. I think he needs to hear it from you. When I try to say this, he angrily sends a quick shiver through my body and then shuts me out. Last time I did this, it took me days and multiple shocks to wake him up.

These days, he spends his time lying on the bed, staring blankly at me. Maybe if you can reach out to him someday and wake him up, maybe he will listen to your voice, maybe he will respond to your touch, or maybe not.

Sometimes, I feel a choke in my throat and a sharp pain in the chest, as if my heart is being continuously stabbed until it breaks into countless pieces. I can hear the crackling sound of those pieces burning inside me. I want to scream, cry, and reach out for help, but it keeps suffocating me and leaves me breathless. No matter how hard I try, I can barely utter a word.

Later, when the night is about to walk away with its blood-coated blade, and the smell of ash starts to fade away with the morning breeze, I am too scared to revisit the moment and write about it. No matter how deeply I dig into my heart to pour my feelings on paper, the words I write are only a fraction of the long, unimaginable struggle, and I know they can never be enough to express how I feel without you.

so many words yet not enough

Hollowness That Twinkles

These stars are dead. Period. I wonder what their names were before someone noticed and named them. Do they know that they have been named after floating in the depths of the galaxy? Do they ever witness the moon shining on the other side of the sky?

Even though they are dead, why does the flicker in them feel like someone squinting to watch me from a distant sky? A different time, a different place, a different person - waiting for me to open my arms. I do that under a clear sky with stars and wait for the galaxy to hit me.

I wish to become a star and flicker like them. I wonder, won't that be lonely again? Will I have another star's company? Do they talk to each other? They all seem so distant, as if they are reflecting me. When one of them is truly dead, I will too. Until then, I wait with my open arms for the galaxy to hit me.

Every night I climb up my roof
and see
which parts of my soul
have drifted far away from me
to become stars in the sky.

Moon

Perhaps it's a terrible thing to write to you. You are just a lone moon hanging over the sky. You don't even have your own light. Your scars remind me of my hollow nightmares. They are so deep and hideous that you have to hide and decorate yourself twice a month. There is a darkness that sleeps in the other part of you. Your whole existence sickens me.

Yet, when I look at you, I'm reminded more of myself than I see of you. The brightness reflects shades of imperfections, battles I have lost, and an unending desire to cling to someone every night, despite the millions of miles distance between my heart and hers.

Though on nights when I sit by the window and stare at the moving cars, I wonder how far you have drifted over all these years.

Probably a million miles away from me, riding with someone to a destination I could never take you, listening to things I could never say to you, and saying things which I have only dreamed of hearing from you.

On a mere imagination of this, the things clogging my throat seep into my eyes and come out from the steep corner. Then, the gaping hole inside me explodes into inconsolable sobbing and shaking of hands, as if in the darkness of my room someone invisible is trying to grab me by my arms and hug me to soothe the ache in my heart.

I wonder what a person can do when suicide is unavoidable

Should he phone each of the people he cared about
and express his gratitude?
Isn't it possible that it will set off a warning
and one of them will come to his rescue?

Should he write a letter to each of them
and leave a postcard in the mail?
By the time they would get them,
he would have left.

What good would these phone calls
or postcards do though?
He is expected to rest in peace
when he passes away.
And in any case,
people would forget about him
in a few days or months.

So instead of disturbing people,
shouldn't he just go to the cemetery by himself?

His time is near, and so I am curious:

Why do people come to leave flowers?
And is there anything he can do to stop them?

I get it.
It's a nice thing to do once in a while.

But I am scared that once they are near him,
his darkness will swallow them up as well
and I don't want another grave next to him.

The only reason he is unavoidable to suicide
is that he wants to be alone and find peace.
"What's a better place to be than in a grave?,"
as he puts it. I wish I could dispute that.

I wish I knew of a place in this beautiful world
where he might find such peace.

Travelled so far, yet not far from you

I used to wonder how far I had to run to not feel the emptiness in my heart. Now, when I can no longer feel it, I wonder how far I have come. I look around and see nothing except the hollow darkness surrounding me and the same emptiness that I used to feel. Strangely, I no longer feel that in my heart.

The objects linked to my past stare at me as if they are pleading for me to open a portal through them and escape to a day in the past. I'm not sure which one, but it had a strange blockade. I push myself hard in an attempt to recollect the past. I touch the object to feel its existence, holding it close like an embrace to the past moments; love, suffering, sacrifice, and darkness.

"I miss her"—maybe it was the tiredness that led my subconscious to mumble to myself. The moment those words left my heart, the blood in my body rushed to stop my heart from daydreaming and my mind from bursting into my broken reality. My eyes are hurting now from fighting back the tears in the corner of my eyes. The sooner those inappropriate words came out of my mouth, the more quickly their existence faded away as if my body is hardwired to not remember someone like her used to exist.

I am slowly sliding back into a night dream, where everything is blurry; at least it looks like that from here. Free of self-conversations, the seduction of those objects, and the vast void in my life without the owner of those objects - nothing seems to bother me here. It's deep black here, with some known and some unknown shadows. Some visions are mine, and some felt like they were stolen from someone else's story. I am here, yet I saw myself living the story as a third person, in a different life, with different choices, different present, and past. I wonder if all my versions in my dreams will ever collide with each other as if the destination was always the same. We would then compare how many objects we have carried with ourselves that remind us of the past.

I personally carry a blanket that is wrapped around my body every night, as if the clutches of my past have imprisoned my soul and my skin is stuck to the fabric of that blanket. Every morning when I come back from my morning run, I see it on my bed. I wonder how early you have left in the morning. I arrange my bed, go for a shower, make my breakfast, and before leaving home, I leave a note for you on the fridge—a random one—hoping today you would come early in the evening and notice it. When I come back home around midnight, I find my home in the same condition I left it, and the note in the same place. I freshen up and go to my bed with the blanket wrapping around my body with a hope that when you come back home, you will sneak beside me, come close to my body, hug me tight and slide with me into my dreams.

Nightmares

And when my eyes stared back
at your blurry image
beneath the moonlight,
in those moments,
I wished I could touch you one more time
to see if the stone in my heart
was ever going to melt.

Earlier, there was
beautiful sky,
ruined villages,
and snow-clad mountains;
and at the corner,
you used to wait for me.

I used to stare, dreaming
how would I feel running towards you
and holding you in my arms.
And when I used to wake up to reality,
tears would travel rolling down my cheeks.

But now—a thick dark cloud surrounds my eyes,
it grips my gaze and takes my attention,

steals me from my bed
to put me in an unending maze.

    maybe you are waiting for me
    on the other end of the maze, are you?

I try to run,
run as fast as I can to find my way back to that
beautiful sky,
ruined villages,
and snow-clad mountains,
and more importantly, to you.

But my legs are plunged in the mud
and my eyeballs—they can't move down
to see how strong it has taken a hold on me;
only thing I feel
is the mud stuffed down into my throat,
suffocating me to my dream-death.

And when I wake up to reality: my lips are dry.
I swallow in the hope of easing my thirst,
everything still looks dark, but familiar to my existence.

I feel grateful to be here out of my dreams,
because dreams nowadays cripple me at night.

From parts of my heart that still bleed and whisper poetry..

I. Last therapy session with her was short:

You must remember:

"A sleep without dreams is equally considered a comfortable sleep. No one takes pills to remember their night dreams. Similarly, you don't need to get your pills refilled to listen to your heartbeats."

II. The time I closed my eyes:

Mornings are calm,
but I feel a blood rush
in my veins
when the clock hits 2 am,
and then I let her
dig sharp pointed nails
into my chest,
and eat out the traces of poetry
from the already dead-stinking-organ inside of me.

III. The first ray of light came at 4:17 AM:

It's almost Monday,
and once more I chose
happiness (she) over poetry.

At once, she felt like a sin,
but soon became an addiction of my heart.
If you cut my heart open,
I doubt you would still recognise it.
You would barely find
a heartbeat in it.

Having a cold dead heart, she claims,
is a blessing.

IV. I think, I will rest now:

I wonder,
once she is done—

which organ would take over
in my hole-ridden chest,
what kind of love
I would have then,
and how soon
she would deprive this new organ
as well of my sad poetry?

Poetry Died In Me

How can I ever write poetry on love
when I am never loved enough by anyone?

How can I ever write poetry on warm hugs
when I don't remember the feeling
of holding someone close to my arms?

How can I ever write poetry on passionate kisses
and intimate touch of two souls
when the intimacy itself
has wiped a part of my soul?

How can I ever write poetry on the excruciating pain
of losing someone important
when I don't remember
either the pain,
or the reason
why that someone was important?

How can I ever write poetry on the possibility
of love blooming again
when I myself don't believe in it at all?

I look at the stars and I hope someday I will also twinkle like them. On my tough days, I often think that I would succumb to my wounds, and it is reasonable to stay in the present moment. But sometimes I think it is okay to look forward to the future—a place where things are going to be okay. Maybe if I keep battling the situations with whatever I have, either a blazing sword or just two words of prayer, one day I will witness something beautiful that will heal my wounds and erase all of my scars.

I think the beautiful thing will be my smile in the mirror or the sunlight resting on my eyelashes for a moment, or it may be something I cannot imagine at this moment. Whatever it will be, I know there will be peace, and my soul would finally rest, a feeling that is yet to knock on my door.

I Want To Bury My Love

I want to bid goodbye
to honour my love for once,
to put you to rest in a place

where roses grow in spring,
lilies blossom in summer,
and the snow greets you
during winter mornings.

But all I can find places in ruins:
ravaged by the firestorm in the past,
and now a thick layer of ashes
is splattered all over.
The sun rarely comes here,
and the rain is afraid to wash away
carcasses of the past.

It feels like a lifetime
since I have been searching
for a place that you might like
to build a graveyard in my heart.

Near The Tunnel

Dark room
Honking horns
Light seeping in

Bloody knife
    Noose around the neck

Screaming soul
Shivering legs
These suffocating nights..

An Open Grave

Yes, I can no longer write poems or words for you. It has been difficult to remember what I had after spending so many nights without you. Most of them seem like a series of beautiful dreams which ended abruptly with the realisation of my reality. It was me who questioned in the middle of the dream. Questions like:

"Do I deserve this?"

"Is this for real?"

"Are you not an illusion?"

They came from nowhere and the answers to those questions snapped me to the place where I am in today. It is the same place from where I had started once. Sometimes I feel like I never met you in reality. I ask myself, were you just an imaginary character in my poems, developed from my disturbed consciousness? Whatever it is, the thread between the reality and the dream has become so thin that I often find myself crossing the bridge in the middle of a random day. The version of me there has taken a shape which not even I can recognize.

It is like, I lend my hand to someone who seemed to be stuck in a well for years. But as soon as I see his face in the daylight, my first reaction is to let him go down that well. His hands were dripping with blood. Every time I pull my hand back, he falls deeper into it than before. I wonder how he had survived such a long period of loneliness and starvation.

It's true that I no longer can hear my heartbeats thumping in my chest. That's why in my poems, I often used the reference of "graveyard" or "a dead heart". The strange thing is that whenever I and the other version of me meet, even if it lasts for a few seconds, I feel more alive than ever, as if someone has planted a living heart in my chest. The love which I felt once comes back in waves, sweeping me away to the deep bottom of the ocean. I could feel the water gushing into my lungs and instead of suffocation, it leaves a calming sensation in my body. Everything I had with you has never been this much crystal clear.

I asked my other version that if my heart is a graveyard, then how am I the only living thing in the middle of it watching all the things I loved getting wrapped in a cloth and then getting buried under the ground? I didn't get a chance to hear what he had to say. But I think it must be related to you or the love I lost.

Then there were a few days when I held his hand a little longer than I should. I heard him, or I remember him mumbling about me. It is weird that he remembered nothing about you. It felt like I was the one who was trapped there in the well. But that made no sense. I would surely recognize my own face.

"Will you?" he asked.

Like a dagger in my chest, his words took me back to the graveyard. There was no sign of love seeping in and love getting lost. Like a fragrance, I could smell your presence but in between the smoke and ashes, it quickly faded away. Almost all of the things that which used to define me once upon a time had a separate nameplate and a few inches of land set aside for their burial.

It was a familiar place. I remembered being here before too. When the pain was too much for me to tolerate, I used to come here and bury a part of it. I thought I could come back again when the storm inside me would settle down, but the dead never returned. I suffocated them inside a casket and laid soil upon them. Eventually I forgot about them and to shield me from being my own murderer, I broke into pieces that should never be glued back again.

The meeting between me and the version of me on at the other side should not have ever happened. I lost him for a purpose. But meeting him means being whole again. I wonder, will I be ever whole again? In the race of battling with the pain, I lost so many parts of myself that I can't even recognize myself in the mirror. I am clearly afraid. In the race of being whole again and to meet my lost parts, I am afraid that someday I will have to wrap myself with the same sheet of cloth and get inside a casket. I could even see a nameplate with my name etched on it and a few inches of dedicated land where I would be buried next. It has flowers seeds sprinkled around waiting for me to be their lifeline.

I look at the bright light of the day outside my window hoping to feel a ray of hope in my life. But unfortunately, I no longer understand what it looks like. Perhaps in the darkness of the casket, I will find the hope to live a peaceful and loving life again. Perhaps I will even find you there with your open arms with a bottle of wine and we would discuss which photographs we would keep for our master bedroom and which ones we would bury like the way we buried our love once. Perhaps.

EPILOGUE

Today I am standing at your favourite place on the shore. The place has no footprints left of our last visit, but I can feel your fingers grazing over my palm and the smile on your face is one happy image that never left my mind over these past months. The sea waves also appear the same. I wonder, the way we remember them, do they also remember us? And if they do, what would I respond when they'll ask me your whereabouts? I would probably say what l have been telling all those people who knew how close we were. Either way, I'll always choose the simple, happy lie over sharing my pain and heartbreaks.

One year ago, this day, we talked about how the sea seems to be happy, overflowing with beautiful waves, on seeing us together. Today, when one wave kissed my toe, she didn't seem sad. Even when she could only reflect only one shadow instead of two, she had the same breathtaking smile she had last year. Every time she touches my toe, posing an additional question, I picked up one of the many lies from my collection and made up all the answers. Even when she caught me lying, and the gloomy look on my face made her doubt my answers, the only thing she did was smile. The same breathtakingly beautiful, adorable smile, which you used to have. I am not sure whether she impersonated you, but that smile, when I think about it after months, had healed my soul.

Acknowledgements

To all the kind souls I met on my page who listened to me and offered comfort—I am indebted to each one of you for supporting me during my lowest times. Even if we never could meet in person, your kindness has helped restore my faith in goodness of the world.

Thank you, Shruti Agarwal, for motivating me at times when I needed it the most and always being sure of a future where my words would find a home in a book.

Shikha Sharma, your friendship truly lifts me. Thank you for guiding my life, instilling patience in me, and reminding me to take pride in the past.

Coming to Bangalore changed my life. I met some of the kindest people: Lisha Jain, Mittali Sharma, Mehul Bhagtani, Rahul Raj, Sneha Wadhwa, Rahul Vishwakarma, Aanchal Agarwal. Thank you all for having me as a friend, keeping me sane and giving precious memories over the past year.

My faith in God is not very strong, but I believe in the universe and moon. I think I would never have made it in this life if I am not blessed with the kind of parents I have. So much love and respect to them for giving me the space in my life.

Looking back, a part of me is also thankful to the person who once sowed seeds of love in my heart. My heart is grateful for your love..

Thanks to my editor, Unnati Agarwal, for agreeing to read the very early first draft of the book.

Lastly, I want to thank you, the reader, for taking out some time to read my words. Your decision to live the emotions and stories within these pages means the world to me.

About the Author

Shubham Singhania lives in Bangalore and is a Chartered Accountant from India. Born in a small town in Bihar, he moved multiple cities to provide for his education and career. He discovered writing as a way to sort through the broken, emotional and overthinker side of him.

'Dark Little Corners' is his debut poetry book and is a collection of poems and proses written during the darkest times of his life. He tries to make sense of this life by gazing at the moon, counting stars, talking to the wind, and deciphering small signs in nature.

A note from his diary:

"I have come very far and started to believe that most days, life is mundane and sad and in between it gets beautiful. 'Dark little corners' is an attempt to find that beauty in this mundane and sad life."

www.ingramcontent.com/pod-product-compliance
Lightning Source LLC
Chambersburg PA
CBHW020723160726
47993CB00006B/2332